EXECUTIVE THINK TIME
Thinking That Gets Results

ELLEN FREDERICKS

&

VAL WILLIAMS

Executive Think Time

Published by Shadowbrook Publishing
P.O. Box 2458
Edison, New Jersey 08818

Library of Congress Control Number: 2003095721

ISBN: 0-9712007-9-3

*To all of our successful busy clients
who inspired us to write this book*

EXECUTIVE THINK TIME

TABLE OF CONTENTS

Introduction

E xecutive Think Time? What is that? Time for executives to think?

Executives are busy, stressed, focused on results, and moving at ever increasing speed. Executives do not have enough time to do what they are doing now. There are downsizings, budget pressures, employee demands, and reorganizations. How can there be time to think?

As executive coaches, we have worked with senior executive leaders from a variety of industries over several years. Our clients have told us in detail what the dilemma is.

Many executives know they are moving too fast. They realize that they don't get enough sleep, they don't exercise as much as they used to, they don't take all of their vacation time, they miss activities with their friends and sometimes their families. They multitask, skip lunch, work late, juggle priorities, and fight fires.

And here is the crux of the problem. Most of our clients tell us that they do not want to work this way but feel they have to. They feel that in today's competitive market place you have to work at this frenzied pace or you will be eliminated.

Senior executives feel they have no choice; this is the way business is, no time to think or plan. Instead, they must be ready, be flexible, and be quick so that they can react to variables that change daily. It is a common assumption that being a high achiever means that you say yes to every challenge, juggle several tasks at once, move fast, and, whatever you do, don't drop any balls.

So, executives work longer hours, push staff harder, reduce personal time. These responses seem to work in the short run. However, the root of the problem remains. Often, both the executive and staff are left wondering what all the activity is about and questioning where they are going.

Even with all the long hours and hard work, people still feel unprepared. Continually trying to get caught up, they are definitely never ahead of the curve. They feel behind the eight ball, pressured to work on things that seem urgent but are not always the most important.

What is missing is the time to think. We call this missing component Executive Think Time. And no executive feels they can afford to take it.

We have a different view. Through our work coaching hundreds of senior executives, we have learned three key things:

1. Executives feel they cannot afford to take time out to "think." We say executives can't afford not to take

the time if they are going to be successful.

2. Executives feel they are already working so hard. We say that taking time to think, Executive Think Time, is actually the real work of a successful senior leader. Executive Think Time is time to visualize, strategize, plan, focus, and align. These are all critical success factors for executives.

3. Even when executives are convinced of the benefits of taking time to think, they do not know what "to do" exactly in that time, what to think about specifically. We have learned that the value is in the inquiry, and we can suggest some specific useful questions. It's not just about the quantity of time spent thinking; it's about the quality and value that gets created from that time. The results of Executive Think Time are the best possible strategies, goals, and actions for your organization. Executive Think Time is about getting results.

So what is in it for busy executives? Why should executives even consider the idea that they make more time to think?

If you are a senior leader in an organization, imagine having even one additional hour to just think about your business. An hour to reflect on what's happening with: revenue, your people, expenses, new products, the organization's culture, productivity, and profit.

We have seen the importance of using think time in this way. Executives who use think time feel more in control, have less stress, do better strategic planning, and are better leaders. These executives do less fire fighting, are less reactive and more productive. And maybe most important, they enjoy their jobs more as they produce better results.

Whether you are a seasoned executive or a new executive, this book will help you:

- See the value of Executive Think Time

- Learn how to structure and adapt Executive Think Time to work for you

- Answer powerful questions designed to challenge you to a higher and broader level of thinking

How To Use This Book

This book is based on our experience working with successful executives. It is intended to offer practical information on specific steps you can take to create high-quality Executive Think Time.

Each chapter presents an important objective and the ideas executives need to put into action to accomplish it. Then we give you the following tools to assess your progress:

SELF-AWARENESS CHECK
Useful questions, specifically designed to have executives get honest with themselves about their current situation. The questions also prompt ideas for action.

THE COACHES' PERSPECTIVE
Comments from us as Executive Coaches on the typical issues and solutions we have seen with our own clients. The brief comments we give are examples of what would be more in-depth coaching customized for a specific executive's situation.

So read the material, actually answer the questions, and start creating Executive Think Time for yourself and your organization.

By the way, we didn't just coach our clients and write the book. We worked the Executive Think Time model ourselves. We answered the same types of questions for our own businesses. We took time out to work the model for our own challenges. That is how we learned how valuable it is.

Client stories throughout the book reflect real client situations however the names have been changed to protect confidentiality.

Mark's Story:
"Fast and Furious" - Behind the Eight Ball

As the Director of Product Management for a mid-sized technology firm, Mark is responsible for current and new product features for the company's hottest product line. Mark routinely works 12-14 hour days plus weekends. Although he works long hours, he frequently feels behind the eight ball. He is constantly multi-tasking and seems to go through the day moving from one meeting to another, usually arriving late. Mark spends most of his time with senior management discussing response tactics for their competitor's most recent market moves or reporting on how things are going. When he does spend time on strategic thinking, he's only thinking about this week, not even the next 1-3 months. He wants to be more proactive about his product line and actually start strategizing and planning for the long term but he can't seem to get out of the firefighting mode.

CHAPTER ONE:
Making The Shift

I f you are reading this book it may be because you are feeling busy but not productive. You may feel that you are not in control of your time or that you just don't have any. Do you feel immersed in details that your staff should be handling? Or are you solving problems that could have been prevented if you had just had some time to think?

Today's fast-paced world values action and results. Both are necessary, but are you spending your time on the *right* actions and focused on the *right* results? If you are reading this book, your answer might be no. So how do you know if you are spending your time on the right actions and results? The right actions come from thought-out strategies and plans, which in turn come from a vision for the future. As an executive it's your job to be thinking about where you want to be in the future – whether it's 6 months, 1 year, 3 years or 5 years out — and creating the strategies and plans to get there.

From our experience coaching executives, we've learned that the higher you go in an organization the more important it is to be strategic. Yet we observe that most executives spend 20% or less of their time on what we call strategic thinking. When you think strategically you are thinking ahead and projecting into the future. You lay out your plans and moves in advance, before taking any action. You not only anticipate what might happen in response to the tactics you plan to use, but you have well developed contingency plans. You are proactive rather than reactive.

When you are tactical you focus on execution. You implement specific strategies, plans, and tactics. Your time horizon is the here and now, not the future. Going deeper into the organization, the percentage of time spent on strategic thinking is even lower for junior executives and senior managers, who are busy with tactical activities, whether they are carrying out plans or responding to the crisis de jour. We believe that it's important for strategic thinking to increase at all levels but especially at the top. While there are no black and white answers, we suggest the following guidelines for the amount of time executives and managers should allocate for strategic and tactical matters:

	Sr. Manager	Jr. Executive	Sr. Executive
Strategic	30-40%	50-60%	70-80%
Tactical	60-70%	40-50%	20-30%

You may be looking at this chart in disbelief and thinking "no way"! You may be skeptical about the importance of Executive Think Time. But if you are committed to increasing your effectiveness as an executive, then it's necessary to make three shifts in thinking about your time:

1. Strategic thinking is equally if not more important than tactical activities and the key to your success.

2. Intentionality, not reactivity, creates desired and sustainable results.

3. You are in control of your time and schedule.

The first step to getting desired results is making the shift to a belief in the benefits of strategic think time. Our beliefs drive our actions, which in turn give us results. Without a shift in belief, you may take different actions but you are likely to get the same results and to expend more effort than required. So accepting that "strategic thinking is equally if not more important then tactical activities" is the first step to getting the results you want. We know that it's easy to get drawn into tactical activities. You often see results immediately. Strategic thinking and planning can be amorphous and do not bring the same sense of immediate accomplishment. So with Executive Think Time, we'll help make the time you put into strategic thinking yield some immediate action and results.

The second step is to make the shift to valuing intentionality over reactivity. Intentionality is your ability to act deliberately: to have desired goals and outcomes, take regular committed action, and manage distractions and circumstances to stay focused on your goals.

The third critical shift that supports intentionality is to see that you are in charge of your time and priorities, no one else. We know that it may not seem that way, but you must start to spend your time on activities that are linked to goals and objectives that you have set either individually or as part of a larger team or organization. Without intentionality, your day will be consumed by other people's priorities.

Executives who deliberately set aside think time are more likely to get the results they want. They tend to be more successful – and less stressed.

SELF-AWARENESS CHECK
Which description best describes your approach?
   a. I spend little to no time thinking about the future but take lots of action
   b. I spend some time thinking about the future and take lots of action
   c. I spend considerable time thinking about the future but take little action
   d. I spend considerable time thinking about the future and take lots of action

THE COACHES' PERSPECTIVE
If you answered a, you're probably in reactive mode. It's likely that your actions are not intentional and seldom linked to strategies and plans. You may not be getting the results that you want. Your first steps are to build your foundation and create the space for Executive Think Time (see Chapters 2 and 3).

If you answered b, you need to ask, are the actions you take linked to your strategies and plans? Are you skilled at managing distractions and whatever circumstances arise? The bigger question is, are you satisfied with the quantity and quality of your think time? If you aren't, then your immediate focus needs to be on optimizing your think time (see Chapters 4 and 5). Even if you are satisfied, what else might be possible if you were to increase both the quality and quantity of your think time?

If you answered c, then you are spending too much time thinking, in "analysis paralysis," and not enough time acting. Your first step is to get into action! Then increase the quality of the time you spend on think time (see Chapter 5).

If you answered d, look to see if you can optimize your think time. Maybe you don't have to work so hard!

Mary's Story:
"Top Gun?" or Not Ready for The Executive Ranks

As the VP of Sales for a large pharmaceutical company, Mary consistently meets or exceeds her sales targets. She works harder than she ever has and gets results but has been bypassed for promotion for the last year. Her performance feedback was very favorable, citing strengths in planning, leading, and execution. Yet a trusted colleague confides to her that she isn't considered a big-picture thinker by senior management. Mary doesn't know where she would find the time to do more strategizing since she is so busy implementing. Besides, she thinks that it's her boss's job to take care of the big-picture stuff. She wants staying power but isn't sure what she needs to do to change senior management's impression.

CHAPTER TWO:
Building Your Executive Foundation™

W hether you are a seasoned executive or new to the executive ranks, you may be working harder than ever and wondering if there is a better way. Or you may be striving to reach the executive ranks and wondering why it isn't happening. Are you frustrated that your people seem to be working at cross purposes rather than aligned towards a common vision?

What makes executives successful is a strong executive foundation. Producing results that add value is a given, but obtaining results consistently requires certain characteristics such as drive, adaptability, resilience, courage, creativity, and focus. Mastering certain executive functions also contributes significantly to an executive's success. Executive Think Time gives you the foundation for the five key executive functions that are critical to success:

1. Visioning

The ultimate objective for the executive is to envision and create a viable long-term future for the business and/or organization. By painting a picture of the future, the executive directs and inspires associates within the organization. A vision is particularly important during times of crisis or uncertainty to keep people focused. Having a vision helps people at all levels know how they fit in and how their work adds value. It's critical to help people set meaningful goals and build alignment within and across organizations. Yet visioning can be challenging for many executives. It's an important but not urgent activity that doesn't have the same immediate payoff as other activities.

2. *Strategizing*

To realize the vision, the executive needs to develop strategies and goals that balance long-term and short-term priorities to maximize results. Think of strategizing as the "how" you get to where you need or want to be and goals as the "what" you are going to accomplish. Strategizing is often neglected because it's easier to jump right into action. The intentional executive anticipates the future by considering "what if" scenarios and keeping abreast of evolving industry dynamics and trends, customer needs, and market conditions.

3. *Planning*

Planning is your roadmap to achieving your results. Planning organizes and prioritizes people's activities and time. It addresses areas such as resources, budgets, timeframes, milestones, measurements, contingencies, obstacles, reporting, and tracking. Good planning reduces the necessity of fire fighting and reacting to rather than anticipating problems. Executives who plan and develop short and long-term goals are more proactive than reactive and appear to be more in control of their future and less at the mercy of changing circumstances.

4. *Aligning*

A savvy executive doesn't assume that people are aligned with the goals and best interests of the company. Instead, you must engage associates and be sure that they understand and are committed to your vision, purpose and goals. To align an organization means to develop accountability and to share ownership of your results. The members of an aligned organization are all moving enthusiastically in the same direction. Alignment is a dynamic rather than static function. Executives need to build alignment every day as business conditions change and people shift within organizations and teams.

5. *Leading*

As a leader at the executive level, you direct, inspire and motivate others. How you do this starts with who you declare yourself to be as a leader. How do you want to be known by others? One way or another, you will certainly develop a reputation, so why not be intentional about how others perceive you? You also create your organizational culture, operating principles and standards. How will you communicate, make decisions, solve problems, reward and treat your associates? What values will you hold and share?

Mastery of these five functions will help make you an executive thinker. There are other functions that are important for executives to master, but we believe that spending focused time on these five strategic functions will greatly increase your probability of success.

SELF-AWARENESS CHECK

Before you can make a shift from tactical to strategic thinking and from reactive to intentional action, you need to be aware of your current beliefs and habits. So stop for a moment and think about the following questions.

How important do you believe these functions are to your personal and organizational success? Rate yourself on a scale of 1 to 5, with 5 being critical and 1 being unimportant.

	Personal	Organizational
Visioning	——	——
Strategizing	——	——
Planning	——	——
Aligning	——	——
Leading	——	——

How much time do you spend each week on each of these key executive functions?

Visioning	————
Strategizing	————
Planning	————
Aligning	————
Leading	————

Are you willing to spend more time on each of these functions per week? If yes, please answer how much time you are willing to spend per week on each function.

	Willing?	Time I Want to Spend
Visioning	_____	_____
Strategizing	_____	_____
Planning	_____	_____
Aligning	_____	_____
Leading	_____	_____

How skilled are you at each of these functions? Rate yourself on a scale of 1-5, with 5 being highly skilled and 1 being unskilled.

Visioning	_____
Strategizing	_____
Planning	_____
Aligning	_____
Leading	_____

THE COACHES' PERSPECTIVE
Importance
If you believe that these functions are important, congratulations! You are thinking like an executive. You can use this book to expand and further optimize your think time. If you don't see the importance of these executive functions, then you are thinking more tactically than strategically and you may find it difficult to carve out time for them. It's easy for executives to fall victim to solving

the more urgent and immediate problems. There is an instant gratification and result that you don't get from visioning, strategizing and planning. You need to re-think what is really important to your success. What might be possible to achieve if you placed greater value on these executive functions? What might you be doing differently? What future results might be possible as a result of your making the shift from a tactical to a strategic approach? Once you have made this shift, carving out the time becomes much easier.

Time
Are you satisfied with the amount of time that you spend on the five key executive functions? If your answer is "yes", congratulations on *acting* like an executive. If you aren't satisfied with the amount of time you are spending on them but are willing to spend more time, congratulations on your willingness to grow your executive skills. To increase your think time, you first need to inventory where you are currently spending your time. What functions do you devote the most time to now? How much time do you spend on email and voice mail? Meetings? Administration? Are these the functions that are going to give you the business results you need? What functions can you delegate? What functions and activities can you eliminate or reduce?

Skill

If you are satisfied with your skill at each function and with the amount of time you spend on each one, you can now challenge yourself for mastery. In what ways can you attempt to master each function? If you aren't spending the amount of time that you should on a function that is a weak area for you, it may be that you are avoiding it.

There are some easy ways to improve your skill. One way is to simply schedule time for the functions that you want to enhance rather than only putting effort into what you're best at. For example, if you are already skilled at visioning but not aligning, don't try and perfect your vision. Instead put energy into aligning key people on your team. Another way to gain mastery is to make weak functions team functions. So if you don't like or aren't good at strategizing, get your team involved in strategy sessions. You'll generate more ideas and probably have more fun. And it's likely that they can use the practice too, so you can all grow the skill together. Is there any action you can take immediately that would increase your skill at a key executive function? Improving your skill will increase your confidence and make it easier to carve out think time.

Bill's Story: "Risky Business"

Bill is a 44-year-old Vice President of Data Services in a Fortune 500 company. Bill was interested in the Executive Think Time model because he was aware that he almost never took time to think ahead. He knows that he's always too busy and that he is not the best time manager. If it's not meetings or special projects, he's doing email or consolidating reports.

Bill values the higher level functions like visioning but tends to avoid them. He just needs to do a better job of making the time. He struggles with working on vision and strategy on his own. Bill finds it vague and hard to show something for the time he's spent, unlike when he clears 80 emails and knows what he's accomplished. He also sees creating a vision as risky, because then you have to sell it, and that's the part he doesn't enjoy.

When Bill is in a meeting with his peers, selling them anything is an ordeal. Everyone is so political. They are more concerned about their territory and how they look than the value of the idea being presented. It's just too much of a hassle.

So Bill acknowledges that he has a block to creating think time—but it's not that he doesn't get the concept. He's stuck on all that he would have to do after he came up with the great ideas.

CHAPTER THREE:
Carving Out the Time

L et's assume you now appreciate all the reasons for and benefits of taking out time to think, plan, vision, strategize. You have made the shift and become strategic instead of tactical and intentional instead of reactive. You are clear on the value of focusing on those higher-level executive functions.

Now, how do you carve out the time? You are busy, really busy, and not just at work. You have a busy life at home with friends, family, personal commitments. And you are a high achiever, so your performance cannot be anything less than outstanding, even while you work on this shift to bigger picture thinking. You might be caught in the bind of not daring to take the time to come up with new ideas, because how would you find the time to act on them?

Reserves
What most executives do not appreciate is the necessity of creating "Reserves."

In order to understand the value of reserves, we only need to look at the average executive's life: one of no reserves.

Many, maybe most, executives are not only working too hard, they are not enjoying their climb up the corporate ladder. The constant feeling of having no time and of being overwhelmed has led many executives to the conclusion that there must be a better way. In short, executives often

37

feel, "This just isn't fun anymore." Feelings of being stretched thin, of being worn out yet up against constant demands, come from having no reserves, no extra time or space.

Let's look at the concept of "reserves." Creating a reserve is creating "more than you need." We are all familiar with financial reserves, and the freedom that we feel when we have enough money to cover unforeseen possibilities. Reserves work the same way in other areas of our lives. We coach executives to create many types of reserves:

- More career opportunities than you need

- More friends than you need

- More boundaries than you need

- More support than you need

- More ideas than you need

- More fun than you need

- More health than you need

In the case of Executive Think Time, we are talking about having enough time to vision, to strategize, to plan.

Therefore, executives need a "reserve of time" and a "reserve of space."

Tools
There are three effective tools executives can use to create reserves of space and time:

- Boundaries

- Daily Habits

- Support Structures

Boundaries
What are boundaries? Boundaries are the limits we draw around ourselves so that we can operate comfortably. Boundaries mark the point at which we decide to go no further.

The ability to set boundaries is the ability to "draw the line." How far do you go? When do you stop? Being able to set strong personal boundaries is *the* core issue of time management. When we coach executives, they always tell us they don't have enough time to do everything. We have a simple, but tough piece of coaching for them: "Say no!" Those two words summarize our entire time management seminar.

And our executive clients give us the immediate push back. This is what we hear: "Oh, you don't understand. All of the things on my to-do list are important. I can't say no."

- "It will impact my performance."

- "I won't be a team player."

- "I might get downsized."

- "If I don't do it, someone else will and take my place."

- "It's part of my job."

- "I'm obligated."

- "You can't say no to family."

- "If I'm really talented, I should be able to do it all."

As coaches, we have worked with executives on all of these common excuses for not setting boundaries, for not saying no. And here is our perspective:

High achievers do not like to admit that they have a limited amount of attention, energy and time. But the truth is there are limits. Therefore, as a leader, you will have to choose which of the many important, urgent tasks will get your attention. This is another leadership skill: making choices. Our clients say that everything is important. You may think that the items on your to-do list are of equal importance. But it is up to you to assign priority. A key leadership skill is the ability to make these decisions: Which items will be done first? Later? Not at all?

High achievers often want to do everything because they feel it somehow diminishes them if they admit they have limited resources (translation: they are human). They often don't realize that excellent leadership is not "doing everything assigned to you." Excellent leadership is making the difficult decision of what you will choose to do and when you will do it with the resources you have. And how do you know which actions are the right actions to take? Right actions are the actions linked to the organization's strategies, visions, and goals.

Saying no to some things is essential if you currently have no reserves. In summary, we have to say no until we reach the point of having reserves. Then we can say yes.

It is saying no and setting boundaries that allows us to create the space for Executive Think Time.

Daily Habits
Think of daily habits as personal standards. They are the things you promise yourself that you will do regularly to help create time and space to plan, to think, to strategize, to vision.

Daily habits are different for each of us, but here are some examples from some of our executive clients:

- Morning exercise for 20 minutes

- Lunch time walk for 10 minutes

- 15-minute coffee break every afternoon

- Weekly pedicure

- Playing tennis or golf twice a week

- Full day off once a month with no agenda

- Weekly massage

What these habits have in common is that they remind us to stop, slow down, and reflect. They help us break away from crisis management and fire fighting. They restore our sense of calm.

Notice that we need to be good at boundary setting in order to have great daily habits. It means when people want to schedule working luncheons, but you have a daily habit of exercising at lunch, you'll be saying no. You can offer an alternative, but you'll be protecting your daily habit time.

Naturally, there may be occasions when you deliberately decide to give up your exercise time. As coaches, we know that this happens. We get that this is part of executive life. The point is that making a deliberate decision to give up something is different than giving it up because we feel things are out of our control. Personal standards remind us that there is a great deal within our control.

Support Structures

Support structures are the people, routines, or things that help us implement daily habits or draw boundaries. For example, many executives use their coach as a support structure. As coaches, we remind executives of their long-range goals, we confront them with tough questions about their choices, we ask about their priorities, we hold them accountable for doing what they say they'll do.

Friends and spouses can be excellent support structures. Executives often get a friend to exercise with every day. A spouse can insist on breakfast together each morning. People working on similar goals often join support groups to keep each other motivated.

Technology is an organizational support structure. For example, PDA's and cell phones can be programmed with timed alarms to remind us to take a break, get a meal, or get to a meeting on time. Similar supports include planning annual vacations in advance, prepaying for a spa or health club. In short, look at what you can do to build in automatic support for taking time out for Executive Think Time.

So, the answer to carving out the space is to value and create reserves by first putting into practice the tools of boundaries, daily habits, and support structures.

SELF-AWARENESS CHECK

Take a moment to answer these questions. How satisfied are you with the following? Rate yourself on a scale of 1 to 5, with 5 being highly satisfied and 1 being not satisfied.

1. I have great reserves in most areas of my life. _____

2. I have sufficient boundaries to support my time management. _____

3. I have all the support structures I need. _____

4. I have daily habits that support me. _____

THE COACHES' PERSPECTIVE

You will each have your own answers to the Self-Awareness Check and we do not know what your specific answers will be. However, we will offer a few quick reminders and things to consider.

Willingness to Create Reserves

If you find yourself having trouble creating reserves, the

question of how willing you are to create them has to be examined. Coming to value the importance of reserves can be a significant paradigm shift. As you can probably guess by now, it requires a good deal of behavioral change. What gets in the way of you creating reserves?

As you start to clarify what the obstacles are, you may need to examine if, for example, you are over promising and then failing to deliver. The behavioral shift you would then try to work on would be to begin promising less and delivering more. So take a look at what is in your control that you could change to create more reserves. Are there situations where you need to say no? What boundaries do you need to put in place?

Hidden Payoffs
Sometimes there is an assumed payoff to not having reserves or to being overworked and busy. Executives can feel that if they are really busy, they look important. They can sometimes think that lots of busy activity means they are adding lots of value. Other executives sometimes think that hard work, even suffering, is a virtue. So if you have no reserves, ask yourself if there is any hidden payoff for you.

Valuing Support
If you are not satisfied with the amount of support you have in your life, ask yourself how much you value it. Do you value a community of people with whom you build

45

relationship? Or, like so many busy executives, are you so stretched for time that relationships have fallen by the wayside?

Once you build a greater reserve of time, you have more opportunity to cultivate and enjoy the support of more friends and associates. Think about how your results might be enhanced if you had greater support. Who and/or what can help you act on your commitment to schedule and keep Executive Think Time?

Approval

Some executives who have difficulty setting boundaries and saying no are actually having difficulty overcoming their need for approval. At the executive level, this is very subtle, not obvious, but the executive knows the truth. They want to be liked by bosses, peers, and subordinates. We sometimes coach executives specifically on getting free of the need for approval and notice that their performance automatically improves.

A variation on the need for approval is the need to "look good" (from a performance point of view). Often executives are doing things specifically not to "look bad" in the organization. This is a natural tendency. However, trying to avoid looking a certain way can skew an executive's performance. Leadership often requires taking risks, being bold. As the old saying goes: "Are you playing to win or playing not to lose?" Often, simply becoming aware of these tendencies in yourself makes it easier to change your work habits and create the reserves you need.

Elaine's Story: "Tunnel Vision"

Elaine is the VP of Marketing for a global telecommunications company. Despite creating a seemingly well-prepared Marketing Plan in a tight timeframe, recent industry events have Elaine's products losing market share more rapidly than forecasted. In addition, her products are suddenly in a declining price situation. Elaine keeps regretting she didn't spend more time exploring the industry and competitive landscape from various angles. If she had, perhaps she would have been better prepared to deal with this sudden downturn. Elaine also wonders if her team asked the really hard questions that perhaps no one felt ready to tackle. By avoiding the provocative questions, she was able to meet her internal deadlines, but she missed the boat on staying informed about what was really going on in the industry.

CHAPTER FOUR:
Asking the Right Questions

A s the saying goes, hindsight is 20/20. Have you ever wished that you could go back and rethink a problem once you had new information? Do you ever find yourself feeling stuck about what to do next because you need more information? Asking the right questions is a powerful tool to help you think more expansively and effectively.

Think of Executive Think Time as exploratory in nature. Exploration, which begins with curiosity, allows you to consider possibilities without having to know what the right answer is or where you are going—something executives are usually paid to know. When you are exploring, you are open to discovering new answers and solutions rather than being attached to particular outcomes. In fact, curiosity requires you to suspend "knowing" and ask more questions. Curiosity also calls for you to view the world from different perspectives. When you are curious, one question leads to another and, before you know it, you are thinking more strategically.

In fact, questions are the key to strategic thinking. We like to say that the answers you get are only as good as the questions you ask. So, the right questions can help you set a course, stay on course, solve a business problem and make better decisions. The wrong questions can take you off track, maintain the status quo when change is needed, and limit your perspective. In business today, it's easy to ask only the questions that give us the answers that we want to hear. Or ask questions that narrow possibilities. However, this often creates blind spots that can't be seen or acknowledged. If you are in a time crunch or in a reactive mode, asking the right question would require more thought and conversation before taking action—something you might circumvent for the sake of time.

So asking the right questions can be a formidable business tool. Executives who know how to ask the best questions not only of others but of themselves, increase their probability of success. Executive Think Time is designed to help you ask better questions so you can improve the quality of your answers and actions, and ultimately your results.

Powerful Questions
So how do you know if you are asking the right questions? It's important that as an executive you ask powerful questions so that you can be sure of getting to the best answers. What makes a question powerful? Powerful questions are generally both provocative and open-ended. They typically begin with "what" or "how". They encourage thought, stimulate discussion, and lead to action. A powerful question is expansive and opens up other perspectives. It allows the conversation to go broader and deeper. Powerful questions lead easily to other questions and invite greater creativity and additional solutions. They also can keep you focused on the future and moving

forward rather than looking backward. That's not to say that looking backward isn't useful; it can be, but only when you are focused on learning from what happened. When you are asking powerful questions you aren't looking to criticize, blame, or find fault with someone.

Powerful questions can be used in Executive Think Time for the following:

Assessment/Evaluation – What's working? What's not?
Visioning – What's next?
Exploration – What are all of the options?
Perspective – What assumptions have I made?
Solution – What are the desired outcomes?
Possibility – What haven't I considered?
History – What led up to where we are?
Learning – What don't I know?

Perspective
Perspective is the lens through which we view the world. Some of us can only see the world though our own lens. Executives who can consider other perspectives are more likely to ask better questions. They might view the problem through the eyes of the customer, the supplier, the strategic partner, or a competitor. For example, you might ask "what does my customer think?" or "what are the needs of my suppliers?" or "what are the objectives and challenges of my strategic partners?"

Warning! Your perspective carries assumptions that may cloud your lens. Often your questions will not be powerful because they will simply validate your assumptions. You unconsciously want to prove that you are right. In the process, you limit the quality and power of your questions.

Your perspective also drives how you approach a situation, which in turn influences the quality of your questions. As leaders, you may be predisposed to asking, "what's wrong?" instead of "what's right?". You see the glass as half empty rather than half full. When asking questions, focus on strengths rather than weaknesses. Start from the perspective of "what's right?" or "what's working?" then move to "what do we want to do about it?".

SELF-AWARENESS CHECK
Answer the following questions on a scale of 1 to 5, with 5 being highly satisfied and 1 being not satisfied:

1. The quality of my questions _____

2. My ability to change perspectives _____

3. My level of curiosity _____

THE COACHES' PERSPECTIVE
1. If you are satisfied with the quality of the questions that you ask, you can practice changing perspectives to see

what different meaning the questions take on and how the answers differ. If you are not satisfied with the quality of your question asking, then practice asking only questions that begin with "what" and "how". This helps to keep the questions focused on the future rather than looking backwards. You can also ask more questions to be sure that you are not limiting your thinking and that of your coworkers.

2. A narrow perspective invites blind spots. Productive thinkers enjoy looking at problems from various angles. Make a habit of playing "devil's advocate" to see what answers emerge.

3. You can never be too curious. Though the saying goes, "curiosity killed the cat," we say curiosity "lets the cat out of the bag". No stone will be left unturned when you value curiosity in yourself and your staff. If you can welcome learning and change you will be better prepared to face and address any problems and obstacles you encounter.

Paul's Story: "Catch 22" - Balancing The Short and Long Term

Paul is the recently hired COO for a training and learning company. He was brought in to help reinvent a business that had lost some of its brand cache. In fact, the company was bleeding in almost all business aspects – revenue, profits, and market share. Paul spent his first sixty days observing and learning and formulating his vision. During this time, Paul got sucked into solving some pretty significant short-term problems that needed to be addressed. It wasn't until the four-month mark that Paul recognized that he was spending more and more time fixing the "low hanging fruit". While he loved solving short-term problems and got great satisfaction from it, he knew that he needed to get back to the bigger picture and longer term issues the company faced. Just how to divide and optimize his time between the short and long term was a problem he didn't yet know how to solve.

CHAPTER FIVE:
Optimizing Your Time

N ow that you know how to carve out Executive Think Time, you may be wondering how best to use it. Productive think time doesn't have to take hours. Nor do you have to abandon or neglect the short term to focus on the long term. Both are important. The Executive Think Time Model maximizes strategic thinking through a combination of reflection, inquiry, dialogue, and diagnostics. The results are focused, goal-oriented actions that lead to planned outcomes.

Each step we take you through has a purpose, structure and result, or output. These steps do not need to be done in an office setting. In fact, you may want to experiment to find the best location. Don't be constrained – your most productive think time might be during a walk in the woods or while you are in the shower. (Isn't that where we sometimes have our greatest insights?)

We also recommend an amount of time to spend on each step. You may want to follow these suggested time frames when you first begin. As you get more disciplined in carving out the time, reserve the amount of time that works best for you.

The Executive Think Time Model has four steps:

Step 1: Focused Reflection

Step 2: Guided Inquiry and Dialogue

Step 3: Directed Diagnostics

Step 4: Targeted Actions

Step 1: Focused Reflection

- Identify key areas, topics
  or issues
- Prioritize list
- Select top five areas

Focused Reflection is your quiet time to think about the issues that have the greatest impact on your business. The output of this step is a prioritized list of topics that might have an impact in the future, which you have identified as needing further exploration. Remember that this time optimally is for strategizing, planning, and anticipating problems, not fixing today's problems. So think into the future. Go out in time at least 6 months, 1 year or 2 years. The suggested amount of time to take for this step is *at least 30 minutes*. Select a place that is quiet and where distractions can be minimized.

Refer back to the five key executive functions—visioning, strategizing, planning, leading and aligning—and ask yourself the following:

What areas or issues need greater strategizing, planning and alignment? Do I have a vision that spans at least a 1-3 year period? Do I have clear strategies that support my vision? Do I have plans on how the vision and strategies will be implemented and by when? Do I have goals that are aligned with the vision and strategies? Do I know who my key stakeholders and customers are?

What external forces will be affecting my business? What internal forces will be affecting my business? What type of leadership do I need to demonstrate in order to achieve my vision?

Once you have the list, prioritize the items in order of their potential impact on your business. Then select the top five to work on in Step 2.

Step 2: Guided Inquiry and Dialogue

- Determine your objective
- Brainstorm for 10 minutes, generating a list of possible questions
- Select the top five questions
- Dialogue and answer each question

Guided inquiry and dialogue is an effective way to identify and answer the questions that need to be further explored for each area or issue identified in Step 1. The output is a list of five powerful questions and answers for each of your top five areas. For planning purposes, you should reserve *at least 60 minutes* for this step. Again, select a place that is quiet and where distractions can be minimized. This step can be done alone, with your coach, or with a group.

Before you generate the questions, it's important to think about the objective that you want to accomplish for each topic, issue, or area. Is your objective assessment, evaluation, exploration, or solution? Once you have the objective, spend 10 minutes brainstorming a list of possible powerful questions that support the objective. Then ask, "What are the questions that I haven't asked or may be avoiding". Add them to the list and re-prioritize. Select your top five questions and move on to answering them. When you are done, you may want to shift your perspective and see how that changes your answers. For example, if you are looking at an issue through your own lens, you want to think about it from the perspective of the customer, supplier, or a strategic partner.

Step 3: Directed Diagnostics

- Review each question and corresponding answer
- Identify any key insights, discoveries, and trends
- Summarize your options and conclusions

By diagnostics, we mean conclusions reached by critical analysis. The purpose of this step is to analyze and reach some conclusions about the answers you collected from your Guided Inquiry and Dialogues. Your output will be new insights you have and trends you discern, which will lead to conclusions. A suggested time for this step is *at least 1 – 1/2 hours*.

When looking at your answers, consider the following:
- What surprises you?
- What assumptions have you made?

- What new information do you see?
- What connections do you see?
- What problem or solution is revealed?
- What's the truth?
- What haven't we talked about?
- What are the contentious issues?
- What are all of the options?

Some results might be:
- You uncover a problem.
- You identify a trend.
- You generate a new idea.

Some conclusions might be:
- Something is missing.
- Our approach needs to change.
- It's time for a decision.
- A new strategy is necessary.
- We are on the right (or wrong) track.

Step 4: Targeted Actions

- List all of the possible actions you can take
- Select and prioritize the actions
- Link your actions to goals

The purpose of this step is to set goals and decide on actions that will move your topic, area, or issue forward.

The output is a plan linking your actions to specific goals. A suggested timeframe is to reserve *at least 1 hour* for this step.

For each topic, consider the conclusions that you have reached. What options are available to you? Now list all of the possible actions that you can take. Select and prioritize the actions you can take that will have the most impact.

The goals you link each action to must be specific, time bound, and measurable. When a goal is specific, it is clear and easily understood, even by a complete stranger to your business. A goal is time bound when there is a date that you will complete the goal by. And a goal is measurable when you have a way to assess that it has been completed. Remember to think about how you will evaluate your actions and results. If you find that you are not achieving the results that you intended, you can adjust your planned actions or add new ones. Evaluating your actions and results allows you to carry what you've learned into other projects and areas.

Congratulations! You've done some strategic thinking. Now you are ready to move into action. This four-step process is simple and easy to use. We invite you to practice it regularly to increase your strategic think time.

Visit the Appendix to see examples of how people have used the model.

Executive Think Time Model

Step 1: Focused Reflection

Identify 1 area to think about (Drivers)

Step 2: Guided Inquiry and Dialogue

Create Powerful Questions (5 of them)

Step 3: Directed Diagnostics

Identify discoveries, trends

Step 4: Targeted Actions

Link actions to goals

Susan's Story: "Sleepless in Seattle"

Susan used to enjoy being an operations executive, but before long her job had taken over. She knew things were out of control when she started doing email at 4:00 in the morning. At first, this seemed to make sense. She had a short commute to her office and realized that if she got up an hour earlier, she could do email before going to work. Then the one hour earlier became two hours earlier, then three. Susan was always fighting a crisis and always on a deadline. Problems seemed to crop up everywhere with customers, the staff, the industry. Somehow without her really noticing, work became her life. Finally Susan's boss realized that they needed to stop and take time to get things under control. As they began working on a strategic plan, it became clear that they had different ideas of the company's vision, so they had to back up and clarify the vision first. It took a while, but finally they had a clear vision and strategy. They sold a less profitable piece of the business and focused on the business that was yielding more. They started having strategic planning sessions once every six weeks and now have become more aligned. They have a long way to go, and lots of plans to implement, but Susan no longer does email at 4:00 a.m.

CHAPTER SIX:
Getting Everyone Thinking

T he Executive Think Time model is a great tool for individual executives. However, the additional power of the Executive Think Time model is how it can move the whole business forward.

Once you begin to use Executive Think Time, you will gain tremendous benefits. However, if you are increasing your own strategic thinking but your staff and your peers are not, you might have a very different sense of the possibilities for your business. The greatest benefits of Executive Think Time come from getting everyone thinking strategically. Otherwise, your own ability to delegate will be limited. If you don't raise the strategic thinking level of your whole organization, it can be difficult to build alignment around your vision. Without everyone thinking at this higher level, you are stuck with limited perspectives and don't get the value of multiple perspectives. If you are the only one using Executive Think Time, the burden will be on you: you'll have to work harder.

If we look at the bigger picture, teams that do not think strategically together do not compete as well. Teams that don't think together have fragmented goals and inconsistent results. They lack innovation and creative solutions.

If your competitors can out-think you, they may be able to out-perform you. So getting everyone thinking at a high level can make the difference between your organization being a leader in your industry or a reactive follower. Imagine if a significant portion of your management team was frequently taking time out to think of strategies for improving the business. What increased productivity, profit, and quality might your business experience?

The opportunity is tremendous. The Executive Think Time model is a tool for pulling out the untapped creativity and imagination of your entire staff, not just individuals. And then, what is the potential for synergy? Combining talents? Teamwork at a whole new level? And what if the entire company culture became one of innovation? What kind of success would be possible for your organization? And how would individual executives benefit from that?

Rolling Out Executive Think Time to the Organization
The first step for sharing the Executive Think Time model with the organization is for the senior leader to work the model personally. Note we are saying "senior leader," which does not necessarily mean the most senior person on the organizational chart. Many of the best initiatives in an organization come from the passion and dedication of one person who can influence others, regardless of their level.

Why is it so important to use the Executive Think Time model yourself before you roll it out to your organization? Because you have to do it, apply it, practice it in order for it to become part of your leadership style.

And as with many aspects of leadership, you can't influence your team to think more strategically if you don't model it. The question of modeling really relates to a larger leadership issue. How do you want to be known as a leader? Are you a firefighter? A great problem solver and crisis manager? Or do you want to be known as a visionary? A strategist? A futurist? People follow a leader more easily when they can see where they are going. If a leader does not appear to have things well thought out, people tend to go wherever they want to go.

So work the Executive Think Time model yourself.
Step 1: Do your own <u>Focused Reflection</u>.
List the five topics that have the greatest impact on your personal business or function.

Step 2: Do your own <u>Guided Inquiry and Dialogue.</u>
Create five powerful questions and answers about each of those topics. Work with a Coach or use your own journal to answer the powerful questions.

Step 3: Do your own <u>Directed Diagnostics.</u>
Come to some conclusions about what it all means.

Step 4: Do your own <u>Targeted Actions.</u>
Set goals and follow up with actions to move you forward.

The reason to do the model personally is to experience its benefits for yourself. When you roll out Executive Think Time to the organization, your own account of how you made it work and how you found it helpful will be invaluable.

People may theoretically see the value of taking time to think, but they can't figure out how to do it, how to get the time. You will be showing them "how" from your personal experience. And your enthusiasm will be evident as you report the results of what you yourself learned through working the Executive Think Time model.

So start the roll out by building interest and building support in your organization. Here are some examples of actions you could take.

- <u>Give a 15-minute presentation</u> at your staff meeting on how people in the room could benefit by using the Executive Think Time model.

- <u>Talk informally</u> to peers and superiors about the value you gained by taking time out to think. Include bottom line results of how it impacted your productivity in measurable terms.

- <u>Create a Pilot</u>. Have an Executive Think Time group session for your own team. Work the 4 steps of the model as a group. Post the results.

- <u>Train people</u>. Once you sell the concept of Executive Think Time, have the organization present short group training seminars for everyone interested to learn the 4-step Executive Think Time model. (See appendix for information on training seminars.)

Benefits for Long-Term Organizational Success
As the organization's management team uses Executive Think Time more, the whole culture starts to shift. The possible benefits we see in long-term success include:

- Less fire fighting

- Lower expenses

- Greater creativity, innovation

- More team work

- Clearer vision/direction

- Less stress

<u>SELF-AWARENESS CHECK</u>
How satisfied are you with the following? Rate yourself on a scale of 1 to 5, with 5 being highly satisfied and 1 being not satisfied.

1. I have personally used the Executive Think Time Model to create valuable action plans. _____

2. I have clearly communicated a vision for my organization. _____

3. All levels of staff in my organization are doing some degree of strategic thinking. _____

4. My management team is well aligned. _____

5. I am confident that my organization will reach its goals in 3 years. _____

COACHES' PERSPECTIVE

If you are not satisfied that you have personally worked the Executive Think Time model to create value, you may want to ask yourself, "What is in the way?" Are you convinced of the value of taking the time? Have you shifted enough to prioritize big-picture thinking? Are you living your boundaries and standards enough to make the space? If not, review Chapter 3. In short, are you walking the talk?

If you have not clearly communicated a vision to your organization, are you satisfied that you have a clear vision? Remember that you can use the Executive Think Time model to clarify and shape your vision. For example, what five powerful questions about vision could you ask yourself?

Creating a pilot of the Executive Think Time model starts with sharing the model with your staff and peers. Have you set a date to roll out the model? You can use the model itself to create an action plan for roll-out: What has to be done? By whom? When?

If you are not satisfied that your management team is aligned, ask yourself what you can do to build alignment. For example, groups of managers can work the Executive Think Time model together. You can use the model in teams to share concerns, conclusions, and ideas for action plans.

And finally, if you are not confident of where your organization will be in three years, ask yourself, "What is missing?" Use the model as a strategic planning tool to create powerful questions about the future. Get small groups of people together to dialogue about the organization's direction and possible future results.

Overall, you want to help the total organization increase the percentage of time they spend in visioning, strategizing, planning and aligning. In many organizations, people look only to the most senior levels for strategic thinking. However, by using the Executive Think Time model at all levels in the organization, everyone's performance is increased.

As Executive Think Time becomes part of the

organizational culture, people at all levels build the skill naturally. Succession planning becomes an effortless part of daily business, since people continually develop the broader more senior skill sets. Working the model together enhances team building and relationships.

What are the possibilities for your organization?

GETTING EVERYONE THINKING

APPENDIX:
Examples of
Working the Model

"Back to the Future"

B arbara, the Director of Technology and Data for a large corporation, used the Executive Think Time model to address typical business issues. Her area was growing considerably, and over the past 6 months her staff had almost doubled, with two new functions being added.

Barbara was concerned that the different managers reporting to her were unsure of what the others did. She felt there should be room for greater productivity and efficiency. Barbara also wanted everyone in the organization to add more value as strategic partners, not just data providers. As the leader, she wanted to create more internal alignment, reduce the silos, and get better results on the annual objectives. Barbara was also working under pressure. The timelines for her area's data results were very tight, and new products depend on her area's data results.

Barbara used the Executive Think Time model in conjunction with her work with her Executive Coach. Here is how she worked the 4-step model:

Step 1: Focused Reflection
Barbara listed the five areas that had the most impact on her operation's success:
    1. Resources

2. People development
3. Common vision
4. Technology
5. Leadership

(We'll use one of Barbara's five areas to demonstrate how she used the Executive Think Time model.)

Step 2: Guided Inquiry and Dialogue

Of the five areas for focus, Barbara started with "Common Vision." In step 2 she created five powerful questions about Common Vision:

1. What is the <u>current</u> vision—and the culture and history of that vision— within the organization?

2. What is my <u>personal</u> vision?

3. What do I want from this vision, and what are the <u>benefits</u>?

4. How will I <u>communicate</u> and <u>implement</u> the vision?

5. What are the <u>barriers</u> to making the vision a reality?

Step 3: Directed Diagnostics

Over a period of a few weeks Barbara spent several short periods (of 1 hour or less) thinking about the five questions and came to some surprising and useful conclusions.

- The most important conclusion was that the word "vision" was a big barrier. Barbara and her coworkers were skeptical about doing "vision work," which they felt was vague and theoretical. In their experience, a "vision statement" usually ended up in a drawer somewhere. It was much more useful for them to give their list of objectives concrete labels such as "Drivers for our organization," "Where do we want to be?" and "What is important for us to do?"

- After thinking about her own personal vision, Barbara realized she did not want to cascade a vision from the "top down." Instead she wanted even the initial vision to start from the managers reporting directly to her and build from the bottom up. So she shifted the focus from her personal vision.

- Barbara also found that the managers she met with all had very different ideas about what was important for the future. Barbara saw that her leadership would be critical to integrate the different functions that those reporting to her oversaw.

- Barbara also concluded that one barrier would be getting her direct reports to think "outside the box." She realized that she would have to facilitate a discussion in which they would question old assumptions and look at the organization from a new perspective.

Step 4: Targeted Actions

Barbara took some very specific actions, based on her conclusions from step 3:

1. She met with each of her direct reports individually for informal discussions and asked what results they considered critical for the organization to achieve over the next 3 years. She didn't use the word vision.

2. Barbara compared the individual discussions she had with her direct reports to look for areas where her managers identified similar "drivers" for the organization. Barbara summarized the similarities she found into one broad theme for the area, which became, in effect, the vision.

3. Barbara developed a step-by-step plan to present this "Summary of Drivers" to both her bosses and peers for further refinement. Barbara also got input from her direct reports on ways to bring the rest of the staff into the loop.

Summary

In the past, Barbara had dismissed the concept of vision for an organization as too vague to be useful. By working the Executive Think Time model she was able to open up to a new perspective, redefine vision, and then use a new approach. In doing so, she took actions that she may not have taken and came to new and productive conclusions. Barbara was also able to balance both short-term and long-term concerns. In her individual sessions with her direct reports, she used their short-term business problems as the starting point for a discussion of where they wanted to be in the future. The short-term crises were the focal point for a much larger conversation.

For example, since the direct reports were very concerned about the lack of resources, both staff and equipment, Barbara asked each of them for their projections of an ideal staffing pattern for the future. Naturally, this conversation then expanded to include future goals, results, and ways of operating. In summary, she helped them create a future vision that involved higher-level strategic thinking yet incorporated their current short-term concerns. Working the Executive Think Time model tied it all together. Barbara had a simple, easy-to-use process that focused her thinking.

"My Brilliant Career"

A lan, the Vice President of Operations for a worldwide corporation, used the Executive Think Time model to think through more personal career decisions. Alan has enjoyed an excellent career with his company but feels he did not plan his career moves. He basically just did his best and took new assignments as they were offered to him. Now in his mid-forties, Alan is thinking more carefully about his next career moves. He has an excellent reputation, so he will have several choices. This time he wants to choose his next assignment based on his own long-term career plan.

Using the Executive Think Time model, Alan worked with his Executive Coach to define his future career moves.

Step 1: Focused Reflection
Alan listed the factors that had the most impact on his overall career development. He chose to focus on three areas instead of five:

1. His current position in the company
2. Alternative positions in the company
3. Opportunities outside of the company

Step 2: Guided Inquiry and Dialogue
Alan looked at the three areas for focus and asked five powerful questions to help him examine his possibilities.

1. What do I enjoy about my current position?

2. What am I best at and worst at?

3. What are my top three values in life?

4. What would have to change for me to be totally satisfied with my career if I stayed?

5. What would an outside opportunity have to offer for me to leave?

Step 3: Directed Diagnostics

Alan set aside brief blocks of time to think about these questions, then wrote down his answers as a way of processing his thoughts. He enjoys using his computer for this type of journal-keeping. Alan came to some interesting conclusions:

*   Looking at things he enjoyed about his job led him to thinking about the type of work he was truly passionate about. He had to acknowledge that sometimes in the past he had avoided certain activities he loved if he felt they had a lot of risk. But after thinking further, he also realized that some of the biggest achievements of his life had involved overcoming his anxiety about taking a risk. One valuable result was that he became more comfortable considering future options that might be risky.

- When Alan thought about the skills that came naturally to him and the skills he needed to work at, he identified one skill he really wanted to develop. Although his interpersonal skills were excellent, he felt strongly that he wanted to be able to "influence others" much more. He also identified an obstacle to influencing others, which was his tendency to sometimes react to political situations when others were posturing or pushing their own agendas. His reaction was very subtle, and not obvious to others, but internally he would become frustrated and annoyed. Having made this important observation, Alan was able to work on staying neutral and not reacting unless he chose to. Alan strengthened his own ability to deliberately choose his reactions; thereby strengthened his confidence that he would not be rattled by others. That critical shift allowed him to be more influential with others.

Step 4: Targeted Actions

Alan identified a few specific actions to take, based on his conclusions:

1. Practice the skill of "choosing when to react" on a daily basis.

2. Build more alliances with a broader range of senior leaders so that he would know more about future job opportunities inside the company.

3. Create a written profile of his ideal job, including its top ten characteristics. He could use this profile to evaluate jobs both inside and outside the company.

4. Write a summary of his vision of a successful life. This vision would go beyond his ideal job to encompass his values, his passions. It would be his idea of what satisfaction in his career and in his life would mean.

Summary
Alan was able to benefit from the Executive Think Time model in thinking about both his career and his life. Alan's example demonstrates that "think time" is useful for many different types of challenges.

APPENDIX:
Key Distinctions

A s a leader, language is a tool that we use everyday to think, communicate, inspire, and motivate. As coaches we are trained to help clients understand the subtleties of language, called distinctions, to create greater self awareness and enhance leadership. In this appendix are several distinctions to help optimize your think time.

Reactive versus Proactive: When we are reactive we are at the effect of circumstances often feeling overwhelmed or out of control. When we are proactive, we stay ahead of the circumstances and generally feel in control. Being proactive is the ideal state for an executive and the primary goal of Executive Think Time.

Intentional versus Random: As executives we are called upon to declare and invent new futures. How we do that efficiently and effortlessly is through the skill of intentionality, our ability to act on purpose or stay the course. The opposite of intentionality is randomness which often results when we are in a reactive mode. As we like to say, "get the results that you want not the ones that may happen". Executive Think Time will help you invent the future and get the results that you want.

Tactical versus Strategic: When we think tactically we are focused on the execution of plans and strategies. Our time horizon is the present. When thinking strategically, we are projecting into the future and determining what plans and actions will produce the results that we need to be competitive and profitable. Our goal when engaging in think time is to stay focused on the future.

Boundaries versus Standards: Boundaries are the limits we draw around ourselves so we can operate comfortably. As an executive it is important to have strong boundaries to create the time to do the most important things in every day. Standards are the personal norms that we operate and live by. They define who we are and how we are known. Make Executive Think Time one of your personal standards and you'll never be reactive again.

Dialogue versus Debate – When creating think time it is imperative to draw out new ideas and viewpoints. As leaders we create the climate to make this happen. A dialogue is an exchange of ideas or opinions. Like a conversation, it can be viewed as non-threatening. People are more likely to share their ideas and viewpoints when they know they will be heard. They are also open to hearing what others bring to the conversation. In a debate, viewpoints are often fixed and the participant's job is to convince the others that they are "right". So when you are engaging in think time with other people, be sure that you are in a dialogue and not a debate to bring out the best of everyone's thinking.

Inquire versus Interrogate: A key part of Executive Think

Time is the ability to ask powerful questions. The way we approach asking questions will set the stage for how willing others are to participate. When we inquire, we ask questions in a way that others can sense our readiness and openness. When we interrogate, we are more intense and we often have a hidden agenda such as searching for information or looking to blame someone. To get the greatest participation from others, inquire don't interrogate.

Optimize versus Utilize – To optimize means to make the best use of. When we utilize something we are using it for a specific purpose. Once you carve out the time for Executive Think Time, the goal is to optimize the think time, not just utilize the think time. It is not about just taking the time. It is about getting the best results from the time.

ABOUT THE AUTHORS:
Ellen Fredericks &
Val Williams

EXECUTIVE THINK TIME

E llen Fredericks, Master Certified Coach, partners with executives, leaders, and business owners to take their individual, team or business performance to a new level. Her company, Partners in Possibility, specializes in supporting clients to build organizational cultures that reflect their vision and values and to develop leaders that can consistently produce new levels of results in the face of rapid change and competition. She also supports clients in the art of building powerful business relationships and cross-functional teams within a complex business structure. Her clients include executives and leaders from start-up firms, not for profits and Fortune 500 companies including AT&T, IBM, Lucent Technologies, The United States Postal Service, Merck & Co., Pharmacia, Schering Plough, Prudential, UniLever, JP Morgan Chase, and others.

In addition to individual coaching, Ellen's professional services include group coaching, facilitation, and workshops on topics such as commitment leadership, emotional intelligence, relationship management, breakthrough thinking, and team effectiveness.

As a former corporate executive, Ellen brings twenty-five years of management and business experience to her coaching from the telecommunications industry where she held diverse positions in marketing, sales, information technology, operations, human resources, and government affairs. Her areas of business expertise include business management, business development, strategic planning, new product development, product marketing, and product management.

Ellen is one of several hundred coaches worldwide awarded the designation of Master Certified Coach by the International Coach Federation. Ellen holds an undergraduate degree in Computer Science and an advanced degree in Management. She attended Executive Management Training Programs at Duke University and Arizona State University.

In addition to her own coaching practice, Ellen is a coaching partner and the Vice President of Coaching for LBF InterCoach, Inc. She is the past President for the NJ Chapter of the International Coach Federation and the Founder and President of the New Jersey Institute of Technology (NJIT) Alumni Association Executive Program Chapter. In 2001, she was featured as a leadership expert for the monster.com Leadership Center. Ellen is a contributing author to the recently published book, "Coaching for Extraordinary Results" (ASTD, 11/02).

Contact information:
ellen@partnersinpossibility.com

V alerie Williams, Master Certified Coach, is an Executive Coach who runs her own company: "Professional Coaching and Training, Inc." Val presents training seminars to organizations and coaches executives individually to achieve career and personal goals. She specializes in Leadership, Strategic Planning, People Development, Team Development, and Stress Management.

Val is a former corporate executive from the Managed Health Care Industry at Prudential Insurance. Val has managed staffs as large as 700 people. Val was Executive Director of Prucare, the HMO of Northern New Jersey; Director of Prucare Customer Service Operations for the Northeast Region; and Director of Group Underwriting, Prucare of New York. Val has managed an annual operating budget of over 25 million dollars with direct impact on a network of 500,000 insured patients and 8,000 physicians and hospital providers.

Prior to her corporate career, Val worked with people on both physical and psychological rehab. Valerie earned a Bachelor of Science from Tufts University and a Master's Degree in Counseling Psychology from Boston University.

Leaders throughout the United States, France, Finland, England and Australia work with Val to raise the quality of their professional lives. Val coaches people (often by telephone) to develop greater focus and overcome obstacles so they design the career and life they really want. In her seminars, Val is known for her interactive approach and practical style.

As a Coach, Val has presented seminars, facilitated management retreats and coached executives and professionals at a variety of corporations, universities, and professional organizations, including: Washington Mutual Bank, Bristol-Myers Squibb, TIAA-CREF, SBLI, General Electric, Prudential, National Utility Investors, American Express, Genentech, Pfizer, Harvard University, Pepsi, Nokia, University of Indianapolis, Horizon-Mercy HMO, AT&T, Lucent Technologies, Delta Dental, Schering-Plough, ADP, Women Unlimited and more.

As a leader in the coaching industry, Val is also a frequent speaker at coaching conferences nationwide.

Val was the first President for the New Jersey Chapter of the International Coach Federation. Val has been credentialed and awarded the designation "Master Certified Coach" by the International Coaching Federation. Val has been featured in many publications including: New York Newsday newspaper, Business Week, Executive Female Magazine, Black Enterprise, Essence magazine and other healthcare magazines. Val has written two recently published books: "Get the Best Out of Your People and Yourself" and "Virtual Leadership."

Contact Information:
Val@valwilliams.com

102

TO ORDER
Visit our websites: www.valwilliams.com or www.partnersinpossibility.com
or Fax 877.443.4092

- *Executive Think Time Training Seminars*
  Ellen Fredericks and Val Williams present on-site training seminars to roll out the 4-step Executive Think Time model to entire management teams. Seminars are customized to the organization's needs. Contact Ellen or Val for details.

- *Executive Foundation Assessment and Coaching Program*
  This assessment shows executives both their strengths and areas for improvement in their executive skills. Then a coaching program is designed for individuals and/or teams to strengthen leadership skills.

- *Other Books and Tapes by Val*
  √ *Get the Best Out of Your People and Yourself: 7 Practical Steps for Top Performance*
  This book gives 7 practical steps for leaders and executives who want to see top performance from the staff. The handbook gives excellent practical instructions on delegation, giving feedback, performance management, and coaching your people. 100 pages ($14.95 + $2 shipping)

√ ***Virtual Leadership***
This little booklet gives leaders lots of tips for how to manage and coach their people when the staff is located in a different city or different country. When staff is in a different geographic location, how do you evaluate performance? coach performance? build a team? have successful teleconferences? This booklet gives solutions. 40 pages. ($6.95 + 1.50 shipping)

√ ***The Ways of Leadership*** (Audiotape)
Strong Leadership is about more than what you "do." Real leadership is built on "who you are." ($10 + $1 shipping)

√ ***Building Your Personal Foundation***
7 Steps for a Happier Life (Audio CD)
Building your personal foundation will show you how to:

Raise your standards
Get your needs met
Eliminate what you tolerate
Restore integrity
Build boundaries
& more! ($10 + $1 shipping)

Shadowbrook Publishing
PO Box 2458, Edison NJ 08818
Fax 877.443.4092 • www.valwilliams.com

Share It With Others

If you'd like to order more books, you can fill out this form and fax it to us at (877) 443-4092, or visit our website to email us and see other products: www.valwilliams.com

QTY	Product	Price	Total
	Executive Think Time	$14.95	
	Sales Tax: (NJ residents add 6%)		
	Shipping/Handling (Add $2.00 per book)		
	Total		

Shipping Address

Name

Address 1

Address 2

City   State   Zip/Postal Code   Country

Phone   Fax

Email
Charge to:

Cardholder name: _____

Credit Card Number   (Circle one): Visa   Master Card   American Express

Expiration Date (MM/YY)

Fax completed order form to (877) 443-4092
If paying by check, mail check and completed form to:
Shadowbrook Publishing
PO Box 2458
Edison NJ 08818
Checks payable to Shadowbrook Publishing

7 Questions -

① What do I eminate as an Unlimited Woman/leader?

② What really matters to me in my work? my life?

. Because of me someonislife is different

③ What differences can I make - right here, right now?

④ Is what I am doing, planning n accepting moving my dream toward?

⑤ What is standing in my way of creating the dream?

⑥ What will I no longer accept?

⑦ Am I capable of transcending all the obstacles?